THE ULTIMATE DAD JOKE BOOK

HUGH MURMIE

TABLE OF CONTENTS

4

Full Groan

How do you know when a dad joke is ready for its debut? It will be full groan. Enjoy these classic, groan inducing morsels of hilarity. You're welcome.

22

Koalaty Trickery

Lacking animal jokes? You've cat to be kitten me right meow! Bear with me through this chapter and you'll bee udderly crabtivating while delivering these top koalaty jokes. They'll be kraken up, no probllama!

38

Eggcellent Wisecracks

Food puns are a gouda whey to pasta time. Lettuce help you turnip the volume on those laughs with these eggcellent jokes everyone will go bananas over!

50

Nerd Alert

Science, Grammar and Math, oh my! Put your thinking caps on and prepare to dazzle even the brightest bulbs in the box with these clever quips.

68

Pop Cultured

Impress your audience with your repertoire of socially relevant gags. Jokes about hit movies, books, international icons and more will make even your most millennial audience think you just might be hip... I mean tight. Fly? Dangit.

82

Play On Words

Ready to take a shot at these gold medal winning sports and games puns I've rounded up? I game to please! Double down on these jokes and you'll knock them outta the park for sure.

96

Punny One Liners

Surrounded by the humorously challenged (or no one at all)? Try these spectacular one liners perfect for a one man show. No questions to be asked or answers to be figured out; you own the whole thing from setup to punchline.

1

How does a one armed man tie his shoes?
Single handedly.

2

What award did the knock knock joke writer win?
The no-bell prize.

3

What sits on the bottom of the sea and twitches?
A nervous wreck.

4

What do you call a person with no body and no nose?
Nobody knows.

5

Why can't an ear be 12 inches long?
Because then it would be a foot.

6

Would glass coffins sell well?
Remains to be seen.

7

What's the difference between a hobo on a trike and a gentleman on a bike?
Attire.

8

What did the policeman say to his belly button?
You're under a vest.

9

How do you get a farm girl's attention?
A-tractor.

10

Why did the scarecrow win employee of the month?
Because he was outstanding in his field.

11

How do you make a tissue dance?
You put a boogie in it.

12

Want to hear a joke about paper?
Never mind, it's tearable.

13

How many apples grow on a tree?
All of them.

14

Why is justice best served cold?
If it were warm it would be just water.

15

Why did the invisible man turn down the job offer?
He just couldn't see himself doing the job.

16

Why did the guy get fired from the calendar factory?
He took too many days off.

17

What do you get when you cross a snowman with a vampire?
Frostbite.

18

How do lumberjacks know how many trees they've cut?
They keep a log.

19

Why did the painting go to jail?
It was framed.

20

What time should you go to the dentist?
When it's tooth-hurty.

What did the cannibal say while eating a clown?
Hmm, this tastes a little funny.

Why are elevator jokes so good?
They work on many levels.

Why did the man fall down the well?
He couldn't see that well.

When is a joke truly a dad joke?
When it's apparent.

Which state has the most streets?
Rhode Island.

26

Why are Sundays only a little sad?
Because the day before is a sadder day.

27

Why did the man get fired from the bank on his first day?
He pushed a woman who asked to check her balance.

28

What does a house wear?
Address.

29

What has one head, one foot, but four legs?
A bed.

30

What's red and smells like blue paint?
Red paint.

31

Why shouldn't you write with a broken pencil?
Because it's pointless.

32

What do pirates say on their 80th birthdays?
Aye Matey!

33

What kind of undies do clouds wear?
Thunderwear.

34

Where do you take a sick boat?
To the dock.

35

How funny are mountains?
They're hill areas.

36 How do you make a water bed more bouncy?
Fill it with spring water.

---

37 What starts with E and ends with E and has one letter in it?
An envelope.

---

38 Why are hairdressers always on time?
They know all the short cuts.

---

39 What do you call a belt with a clock on it?
A waist of time.

---

40 Why was the bed wearing a disguise?
It was under covers.

51

Why do you go to bed?
The bed won't come to you.

52

What 2 questions are impossible to answer with "yes"?
Are you asleep? Are you dead?

53

Why can't towels tell silly jokes?
They have a dry sense of humor.

54

What does an apple a day keep away?
Anyone, as long as you throw it hard enough.

55

What should you do if you are being attacked by clowns?
Go for the juggler.

56

Why should you hold the door open for a clown?
It's a nice jester.

57

What do you call a sleepwalking nun?
A Roamin Catholic.

58

How do plants comfort each other when they are sad?
They photosympathize.

59

Why can't you make reservations at libraries?
They are always completely booked.

60

What do lawyers wear to court?
Lawsuits.

81

What genre of music do national anthems belong in?
Country music.

82

Why should you never iron a four leaf clover?
You don't want to press your luck.

83

What do you call an indecisive beach?
I'm not shore.

84

How did the inventor of ballet skirts figure out what
to name them?
She put tu and tu together.

85

Why did the plumber quit his job?
It was too draining.

86 Why couldn't the lumberjack think of a good tree pun?
He was stumped.

87 What to you become when reading while sunbathing?
Well red.

88 Did you know toasters aren't waterproof?
I was shocked!

89

What do you call a bear with no teeth?
A gummy bear.

90

Why don't you ever see elephants hiding in trees?
Because they're so good at it.

91

How many tickles does it take to make and octopus laugh?
Ten tickles.

92

Why do penguins carry fish in their beaks?
They don't have any pockets.

93

What do you get from a fancy, pampered cow?
Spoiled milk.

94

Why do bees have sticky hair?
The use honey-combs.

95

What do you call a dog magician?
A labracadabrador.

96

What do you call a deer with no eyes?
No idea.

97

What did the buffalo say to his son when he left for work?
Bison.

98

Why don't crabs ever share their toys?
Because they are shellfish.

109 What do you call two octopuses that look the same?
Itenticle.

110 Why did the fish get bad grades?
He was below sea level.

111 Where does a sick fish go?
To see a sturgeon.

112 What does the Loch Ness monster eat?
Fish-n-ships.

113 What do you call a fish who doesn't believe in war?
A pacifish.

114

Who was the best employee in the ocean's balloon factory?
The blowfish.

115

Why should you never pick a fight with a squid?
They are well armed.

116

How do you get a message to a fish?
Drop it a line.

117

Where can you find a crab with no legs?
Exactly where you left it.

118

What do you call a lazy kangaroo?
A pouch potato.

119

What kinds of horses only come out after the sun sets?
Nightmares.

120

What do you call a pig doing karate?
Pork chop.

121

What do you call an owl that can do magic tricks?
Hoooodini

122

Why do ducks have tail feathers?
To cover their bum quacks.

123

Why are teddy bears never hungry?
Because they are always stuffed.

124

What do you call a bear with no ears?
B.

125

What day of the week to chickens hide?
Fry-day.

126

What's the difference between a weird rabbit and an athletic rabbit?
One is a bit funny and the other is a fit bunny.

127

What do you call an ant that won't go away?
PermanAnt.

128

Where do sheep go for a haircut?
The Baa Baa Shop.

139

Why are wasps so unpopular with other bugs?
They are just wannabees.

140

What do you call a fly with no wings?
A walk.

141

What do you call a bee who is always complaining?
A grumble bee.

142

Why is a chicken soccer match a bad idea?
There are too many fowls.

143

What are the dangers of walking when it's raining cats and dogs?
You might step in a poodle.

144

What is a snake's favorite subject in school?
Hiss-tory.

145

What did the judge say when the skunk walked in the courtroom?
Odor in the court!

146

Why do fish live in salt water?
Pepper water would make them sneeze.

147

What do you get when you cross an elephant with a fish?
Swimming trunks.

148

What kind of birds stick to everything?
Vel-Crows.

149

Where do cows display their artwork?
At the Moo-seum.

150

What do you call a seagull flying over a bay?
A bagel.

151

How do snails fight?
They slug it out.

152

Why are penguins socially awkward?
They don't want to break the ice.

153

What do you call a cow in an earthquake?
A milkshake.

154

Why aren't koalas counted as real bears?
They don't meet the koalafications.

155

What sound do porcupines make when they hug?
Ouch!

156

Why can't leopards hide?
They are always spotted.

157

What happens to illegally parked frogs?
They get toad.

158

What did the duck say when he bought chapstick from the hotel desk?
Put it on my bill.

164

What happened when the cheese factory exploded?
Da brie was everywhere.

165

What do nosey peppers do?
Get jalapeño business.

166

Did you know the first french fries weren't even made in France?
They were cooked in Greece.

167

What do vegetarian zombies eat?
Graaaaiiinnnsss.

168

Why did the banana go to the doctor?
He wasn't peeling well.

169

What do you say to a salad that is freaking out?
Please romaine calm.

170

What happened to the girl they interrogated for the stolen panini sandwich?
They really grilled her.

171

What is the most lonely kind of cheese?
Provolone.

172

What is orange and sounds like a parrot?
A carrot.

173

What did the ranch say when someone opened the fridge door?
Close the door! I'm dressing!

174

What do you call a fake noodle?
An impasta.

175

What do you call cheese that isn't yours?
Nacho cheese.

176

Why can't eggs tell jokes?
They'd crack themselves up.

177

Did you hear the awful rumor about butter?
Wait, we shouldn't spread it.

178

What is a happy cowboy's favorite candy?
Jolly Ranchers.

179

Why did the tomato blush?
It saw the salad dressing.

180

What's the best snack to eat during a scary movie?
I scream.

181

When do you stop at green but go on red?
When eating a watermelon.

182

How much room is needed for fungi to grow?
As mushroom as possible.

183

How do you know carrots are good for your eyes?
You never see a rabbit wearing glasses.

184

How do you make an eggroll?
You push it.

185

What do you call the new girl at the bank?
Nutella.

186

How do you fix a broken pizza?
Tomato paste.

187

What has bread on both sides and is afraid of everything?
A chicken sandwich.

188

What did the nut say when he sneezed?
Cashew!

189

What do you get when you step on a grape?
A little whine.

190

What's long, green, and slowly turning red?
A cucumber holding its breath.

191

What do you give a hurt lemon?
Lemon aid.

192

How to you fix a broken pumpkin?
With a pumpkin patch.

193

What kind of fruit can fix your sink?
A plumber.

194

Why did the orange go out with the prune?
He couldn't find a date.

195

Why did the guy lose his job at the orange juice factory?
He couldn't concentrate.

196

What do you call an apple that plays the trumpet?
Tooty fruity.

197

Why should you never tell a secret in the produce aisle?
Corn have ears, potatoes have eyes and beanstalk.

198

What is a pretzel's favorite dance?
The twist.

199

Where does spaghetti go to dance?
The meatball.

200

What do you call an almond in a spacesuit?
An astronut.

201

Why can't you use 'beefstew' as a password?
It's not stroganoff.

202

Why is milk the fastest drink on earth?
It's pasteurized before you ever see it.

203

What is a ghost's favorite pie?
Boo berry.

204 What's worse than finding a worm in your apple after you take a bite?
Finding half of a worm.

205 What are the two things you can never have for breakfast?
Lunch and dinner.

206 Why did the girl throw butter out the window?
She wanted to see a butterfly.

207 How many apples can you fit in an empty box?
One. After that one it's not empty anymore.

208 What room has no windows, floor, walls or roof?
A mushroom.

209

How did the church advertise their fish fry?
Our Cod is an awesome Cod!

210

What does a banana say when it answers the phone?
Yellow?

211

Why did the cookie go to the doctor?
He was feeling crummy.

212

How do you make fruit punch?
Give them boxing gloves.

213

What side of a coconut has the most hair?
The outside.

Have you heard about the new restaurant on the moon?
Decent food, but no atmosphere.

Have you read the book about anti-gravity?
It's impossible to put down!

What is an astronaut's favorite part of a computer?
The space bar.

Why was the math book so sad?
It had a lot of problems.

Why can't you trust an atom?
They make up everything.

229

Who was the most round knight in King Arthur's court?
Sir Cumference.

230

What does it sound like to bounce a 747?
Boeing, Boeing, Boeing

231

Have you heard of the new band 1023MB?
They're okay, but they don't have a gig yet.

232

Someone said they weighed less than a thousandth of a gram.
Seriously, like 0MG.

233

Want to hear a time travel joke?
Never mind, you didn't like it.

234

Why are spiders so smart?
They can find anything on the web.

235

Where do dads store their best dad jokes?
In their dad-a-base.

236

How do you organize a space party?
You planet.

237

How do you put a baby alien to sleep?
You rocket.

238

What happens when someone steals uranium?
It becomes theiranium.

239 Why is justice best served cold?
If it were warm it would be justwater.

240 What's the best time on the clock?
6:30, hands down.

241 How do trees get on the internet?
They log in.

242 Why don't computer keyboards ever sleep?
They have two shifts.

243 Why can't you run through a camp ground?
You can only ran, because it's past tents.

254

What is a computer's favorite dance?
Disco.

255

How did the dad answer his son when he asked if they were pyromaniacs?
Yes, we arson.

256

What happened to the car with an engine made of wood?
It wooden go.

257

What happens if you swallow a dictionary?
You'll get thesaurus throat you've ever had.

258

What ten letter word starts with gas?
Automobile.

259

What does a thesaurus eat for breakfast?
A synonym roll.

260

How many seconds are in a year?
12: January 2nd, February 2nd...

261

How do you get straight A's?
With a ruler.

262

What is a pirate's favorite subject?
Arrrrrrrt.

263

How to bees get to school?
On the school buzz.

264

Why didn't the sun go to college?
Because it already has like a million degrees.

265

Why do cafeteria clocks run slow?
They always go back four seconds.

266

What do you call someone with a dictionary in their back pocket?
Smarty pants.

267

Why do rocks in space taste better than rocks on earth?
They are a little meteor.

268

What do you call an apology written with dots and dashes?
Remorse code.

Why couldn't the under age angle get a loan?
His parents wouldn't cosine.

Why did the obtuse angle go to the beach?
Because it was over 90 degrees.

What do you call a mathematician who spent all summer in the sun?
A tangent.

What did the geometry teacher say when her curse was cured?
My hexagon!

What do you call a dead parrot?
Polygon.

284

How many programmers does it take to screw in a light bulb?
None, that's a hardware problem.

285

What is the best sport in Minecraft?
Boxing.

286

What did the photon say when asked if she had baggage to check at the airport?
No bags, I'm traveling light.

287

What kind of music do planets listen to?
Neptunes.

288

If the Silver Surfer and Iron Man were on the same side, what would they be called?
Alloys.

289 Why was the music student kicked out of school?
For taking notes.

---

290 White knight of the round table was the protector of foods?
Sir Anwrap.

---

291 When is it the hardest to get rid of debt?
When you can't budge it.

---

292 Why do optometrists live longer?
Because they dilate.

---

293 What does a rusty can of rust remover smell like?
Irony.

294

Where do bad rainbows go?
Prism.

295

Why don't ants ever get sick?
They have anty bodies.

296

What's the best way to carve wood?
Whittle by whittle.

297

Why is the collected works of Shakespeare heavier than a prison full of inmates?
The prose outweighs the cons.

298

Why did the pregnant woman shout, "Couldn't, wouldn't, can't, didn't!?"
She was having contractions.

299

Why did Shakespeare only write in ink?
Pencils confused him; 2B or not 2B?

300

What's the only word that becomes shorter when you
add two letters to it?
Short.

301

Did you hear about the reality show where flat earthers
trying to find the edge of the world?
It was boring; there weren't any cliffhangers.

302

What would happen if Americans switched from
pounds to kilos overnight?
There would be mass confusion.

303

What kind of fishing bait do librarians use?
Book worms.

How can you tell if a Pokemon across the room thinks you are cute?
He keeps trying to Pikachu.

What is Salvador Dali's favorite breakfast food?
Surreal.

What is a chiropractor's favorite music?
Hip Pop.

What did the drummer name his twin daughters?
Anna One, Anna Two.

How did Darth Vader know what Luke got him for Father's Day?
He felt his presents.

313

If you see a crime at an Apple store, what are you?
An iWitness.

314

What do you call a $3 apple pie in Jamaica and a $5 cherry pie in Aruba?
The pie rates of the Caribbean.

315

If FedEx and UPS got tired and merged, what would they be called?
FedUP

316

Who is in charge of Atheists?
No one. It's a non-prophet organization.

317

What concert only costs 45 cents?
50 cent with Nickelback.

318

What kind of shoes do spies wear?
Sneakers.

319

What's the best thing about Switzerland?
I'm not sure, but the flag is a huge plus.

320

What was Beethoven's favorite fruit?
Ba-na-na-naaaa.

321

What is E.T. short for?
Because he has tiny legs.

322

Why is Peter Pan always flying?
Because he Neverlands.

323

What do you call the Terminator when he retires?
The Exterminator

324

Why are celebrities so cool?
They have a lot of fans.

325

Why are Russian dolls so stuck up?
They are full of themselves.

326

What did the guy say who got hit in the head with a can of Sprite?
I'm fine, it was a soft drink.

327

Which US state has the smallest soft drinks?
Minnesota.

What rock group of 4 guys doesn't sing at all?
Mount Rushmore.

What do you call the security guards working at Samsung?
Guardians of the Galaxy.

Why didn't Dorothy know Glenda was the good witch?
She didn't know which witch was which!

Have you seen the new movie about the hot dog?
I hear it was an Oscar Weiner.

What do you get when you cross a robot with a tractor?
A transfarmer.

343

Why did the angry Jedi cross the road?
To get to the Dark Side.

344

What do you call 5 Sith troopers piled together on a lightsaber?
A Sith-kabob.

345

Why did Star Wars episodes 4-6 come before 1-3?
In charge of directing, Yoda was.

346

Why did Professor Snape stand in the middle of the road?
So no one would know what side he was on.

347

Why can't Harry Potter tell his potions pot from his best friend?
They are both cauldron.

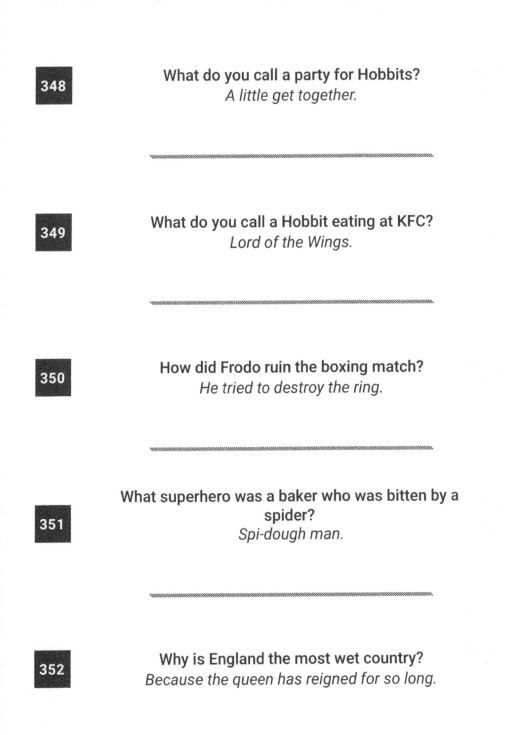

348

What do you call a party for Hobbits?
A little get together.

349

What do you call a Hobbit eating at KFC?
Lord of the Wings.

350

How did Frodo ruin the boxing match?
He tried to destroy the ring.

351

What superhero was a baker who was bitten by a spider?
Spi-dough man.

352

Why is England the most wet country?
Because the queen has reigned for so long.

353

Why couldn't Dracula's wife get any sleep?
Because of his coffin.

354

How did the hipster burn his tongue on his pizza?
He ate it before it was cool.

355

What do you call it when Batman skips out on church?
Christian Bale.

356

What do you say to Simba when he's moving too slow?
Mufasa!

357

What do you call a droid who takes the long route?
R2Detour

Where does Captain Hook go shopping?
Second hand stores.

What do you call paying $1000 to rent a limo with no driver?
Spending a lot of money with nothing to chauffeur it.

How can you tell if Legoland is busy?
People will be lined up for blocks.

Did you see the stage production about puns?
It was a great play on words.

Why is running with bagpipes dangerous?
You might trip and be kilt.

373

How do you cut Rome in half?
With a pair of Caesars.

374

What do you call a bacon wrapped dinosaur?
Jurassic Pork.

375

Why wasn't Infinity War a vegan movie?
Everything was at steak.

376

What do you call delivery birds who like rap music?
Homie Pigeons.

377

Why couldn't the bicycle stand up?
It was two-tired.

378

Did you hear about our crazy camping trip?
It was in tents.

379

What's the best way to watch fly fishing tournaments?
Live stream TV.

380

Why don't sprinters eat anything before they race?
Because they fast.

381

Why would you play soccer if you weren't that good at it?
Just for kicks.

382

I needed some exercise so I decided to take up fencing.
The neighbors threatened to call the police if I didn't put it back.

383

Why should you never marry a tennis player?
Love means nothing to them.

384

Why do golfers always have an extra pair of pants?
In case they get a hole in one.

385

What do you call it when four bullfighters fall into quicksand?
Quatro Sinko

386

What do you call a boomerang that doesn't work?
A stick.

397

What has 18 legs and catches flies?
A baseball team.

398

Why are basketball players such messy eaters?
They're always dribbling.

399

Why don't basketball players go on vacation?
They're not allowed to travel.

400

What does a basketball player do if he loses his sight?
Become a referee.

401

What do you call 12 millionaires watching the NBA Finals together?
The Detroit Pistons (or your audience's favorite team).

402

What do you call the Cleveland Browns (or your audience's favorite team) at the Super Bowl?
Spectators.

403

Why do football players date smart women?
Because opposites attract.

404

Which hockey player wears the biggest helmet?
The one with the biggest head.

405

What do you call the greatest hockey player who decided not to play hockey?
Wayne Regretzky.

406

Where do hockey players get most of their money?
From the Tooth Fairy.

427

What do a boxer, music producer and fisherman all need?
The right hook.

428

Why did the bike run the same people over every day?
It was a vicious cycle.

429

You've never tried blindfolded archery?
You don't know what you're missing.

430

Why do ballet dancers change their routine right before performances?
To keep them on their toes.

431

What is a cheerleaders favorite kind of dog?
A pom-pomeranian.

432

How many dancers does it take to change a light bulb?
Five, six, seven, eight!

433

What did the ballerina say when she couldn't find her ballet shoes?
This is pointless!

434

What was the dancer feeling after 6 hours of rehearsal?
The agony of de-feet.

435

Why was the tiny ghost invited to be on the volleyball team?
They just needed a little team spirit.

436

Why was the magician so great at ice hockey?
He always pulled a hat trick.

437

Why do hockey players work at bakeries in the off season?

They are great at the icing.

438

How many golfers does it take to change a light bulb?

FORE!

439

What do bears call campers in their sleeping bags?

Soft tacos.

440

Why didn't the hunter buy a camouflage tent?

He couldn't find any.

441

What do you call an escaped inmate going camping?

Criminal intent.

When does a British tennis match end?
When it's Wimble-done.

How did Scrooge get a football?
The ghost of Christmas passed.

What is the soccer field on the moon made of?
Astro turf.

Why was the golfer crying?
He was going through a rough patch.

I only know 25 of letters of the English alphabet.
I don't know why.

My mom asked me to clear the table.
It took a running start, but I totally made it!

I know a lot of jokes about retired people.
None of them work.

I'm suspicious of trees on sunny days.
They just seems a little shady.

I told my girlfriend she drew her eyebrows too high.
She looked surprised.

461

I wanted to exercise so I went to the gym and hopped on a treadmill.
I got some funny looks so I started jogging instead.

462

I was wondering why the baseball kept getting bigger.
And then it hit me.

463

I love bowling puns.
They're right up my alley.

464

I used to be scared of running hurdles.
But I got over it.

465

The fish had a girlfriend for a while but he lobster.
Then he flounder.

466

If you have any fish puns...
Just let minnow.

467

My wife discovered that I replaced our bed with a trampoline.
She was so mad she hit the roof.

468

I can't believe my neighbor knocked on my door at 3AM!
Luckily I was already awake practicing my bagpipes.

469

I wanted to tell a carpentry joke.
I couldn't find any that woodwork.

470

Astronomers got really tired of watching the sun come around the earth every 24 hours.
So they just called it a day.

471

The inventor of the umbrella wanted to call it a "brella."
But he hesitated.

472

Don't argue with me about which vowel is the best.
I will always win.

473

What's that vegan girl's name?
I swear I've seen herbivore.

474

I watched a show about how boats are held together.
It was riveting.

475

I was robbed by 6 dwarves!
Not Happy.

486

My mood ring is missing.
I don't know how I feel about it.

487

I tried to grab the fog.
I mist.

488

A book fell on my head.
I only have my shelf to blame.

489

My recliner is one of my best friends.
We go way back.

490

I accidentally ate cat food.
Don't ask meow.

491

My wife gets on my case for not knowing how to season food properly.
I don't mind though, I take it with a grain of sugar.

492

I don't trust French food.
It gives me the crepes.

493

I always think adding more herbs will help my cooking.
But I'm wrong thyme and thyme again.

494

You really gotta hand it to all the short people out there.
Seriously, they can't reach it.

495

To ride a horse, or not to ride a horse.
That is equestrian.

496

Yesterday I was surprised to learn I was colorblind.
The news really came out of the purple.

497

I went to a very emotional wedding.
Even the cake was in tiers.

498

I was given some gloat cream for my bragging problem.
I can't wait to rub it in.

499

My fat parrot died.
I'm sad, but it's a huge weight off my shoulders.

500

My son will only play electronic dance music.
He won't techno for an answer.

501

I submitted 10 puns in a joke contest to see if one would win.
No pun in ten did.

Congratulations! You've made it to the end. Hopefully you had a gut-busting time making your way through this book of hilarity. Be sure to check back in at least weekly to keep your joke game strong. Remember, seven days without a pun makes one weak.

Made in the USA
Monee, IL
16 June 2022

98152909R00059